# Fruitful Friends:
# Filled with the Spirit

But the fruit of the Spirit is love, joy, peace, patience, kindness, goodness,
faithfulness, gentleness, and self-control.
*Galatians 5:22-23*

## Written by Dana Orr
## Illustrated by Ellen Abramo

♡, Ellen Abramo

Fruitful Friends, LLC

ISBN-10: 0-9835635-0-0
ISBN-13: 978-0-9835635-0-1
Library of Congress Control Number: 2011927782

# Dedication

We would like to dedicate this book to our husbands,
children, and all of our friends and family who have shown
the fruit of the Spirit to us.

Manufactured within CPSIA guidelines
Printed by Four Colour Print Group
Printed in China
06/11/2011
Batch #1

*A portion of the proceeds from Fruitful Friends books and merchandise
will be donated to carefully selected charitable organizations.*

Fruitful Friends, LLC
For more information and fun activities, visit our Web site:
www.fruitfulfriends.com

# What people are saying about *Fruitful Friends: Filled with the Spirit*

- Dana Orr has been a "Fruitful Friend" to me. Her walk with Jesus Christ has born fruit in a book for children that I recommend . . .
    Rob Evans, The Donut Man (www.donutman.com)

- Fill your child with the Spirit and with healthy foods.
    William Sears, M.D. (www.askdrsears.com)

- May each of our children be filled with His Spirit—this book will be a great guide.
    Sara Eggleston, author, *On Eagle's Wings*

- This is an amazing biblical story that all children need to hear . . . wish I had it when my children were young.
    Mary Lynn Poe, mother, Virginia

- Martin Luther King, Jr. said that it is the content of a person's character that matters. I know this book will teach our children the way to LIVE not just exist!
    Reggie Dabbs, motivational speaker (www.reggiedabbsonline.com)

- We all find out that we need fruit. The body and the spirit. This introduces this core value to children early in their lives.
    Frank Eggleston, D.D.S.

- There are two stories we can nurture and grow our children with . . . the first is the story of scarcity, the second is abundance. Life to the full is available to those blessed with the fruit of the Spirit.
    Jeff Olson, retired U.S. Olympian, father of three daughters

- Amazing for Life!
    Bear Grylls, Everest mountaineer, best-selling author, international speaker (www.beargrylls.com)

We eat *fruits* and veggies so our bodies will stay healthy and strong every day.
But, the *fruits of the Spirit* you cannot eat; they come from God as a special treat.

There are nine of these *fruits* to be
planted inside.
They serve us, as our thoughts, words,
and actions they guide.

We ask for each *fruit* to be granted as a gift,
so to God our humble prayers we uplift.
With the *fruits* in our hearts everyday,
we can serve our neighbors in a wonderful way.

***Charity***, God tells us is best.
Putting others before ourselves is
the test.

***Joy*** is when our hearts are full of glee,
Knowing God loves us, happy we will be!

**Peace** is when we feel quiet and calm,
like snuggling while
reading with Dad or Mom.

***Patience*** is when we wait
without bugging.
Our turn comes without pushing or
tugging.

***Kindness*** is to our friends being nice.

It pleases God when we serve up a slice!

***Goodness*** is choosing what is right.
With God's help, bad choices we fight.

**_Faithfulness_** is when we believe with our heart,
That God is with us, never to be apart.

***Gentleness*** is not being rough,
with words, friends, and even our stuff.

**Self-control** is when we stop when tempted to be bad, and pray for thoughts, words, and actions that will make God glad.

So now we have learned how
to serve our neighbors best.
Don't let the *fruits of the Spirit* rest.
Plant them inside you so they will grow,
and go out and share them with
everyone you know!

# Acknowledgments

We would like to thank the Holy Spirit for inspiring our friendship, for the privilege to spread His message of Love, and for the journey that our families are on together. And, in addition: Steve Wood and Lucy Allen for their advice; Tabby House for helping us bring this book to fruition; Virginia Culbertson for her assistance in editing; our husbands for getting this book "off the ground"; our friends and family for their continued support and encouragement; our faithful endorsers, and all the families who purchase this book . . . may it be an instrument in your spiritual journey as it continues to be in ours.